The ROAD *to Amazing*

basics of christian practice

Leader Guide

Clayton Oliphint
and
Mary Brooke Casad

Abingdon Press
Nashville

CONTENTS

INTRODUCTION

For many centuries, the word *journey* has been used when describing the life of a follower of Jesus. It is a word that helps us understand that being a Christian is not reaching a fixed point—rather, we are walking the road that leads to salvation and freedom, striving to follow the example of Christ. The journey is not always smooth or easy, but it is filled with remarkable moments of insight and blessing. Along the way, Jesus shows up and surprises us. He is our traveling companion, walking the road with us, even when we are not aware of his presence.

In focusing on the basics of Christian practice in *The Road to Amazing*, readers will learn the significance of baptism as the starting point of a Christian's journey. They will be confronted with the question "Who is Jesus?" and reflect on the cost of discipleship and what that can mean for our daily lives. Like Zacchaeus, they will experience what a difference Christ's transforming love can make in their lives. And, as those early disciples on the road to Emmaus discovered on the very day Christ was resurrected, they will learn to recognize how Christ comes to us and walks with us in all of life's joys and sorrows.

Each of the chapters in *The Road to Amazing* draws on a story from the Gospel of Luke. As you lead discussion on each chapter, you may want to have some working knowledge of Luke's Gospel. We suggest that you read through the entire book to get an overview of how Luke tells us the story of the life, death, and resurrection of Jesus. (See "Background on the Gospel of Luke," pages 13–14 in this guide for additional information.) The four stories from Luke's Gospel included in *The Road to Amazing* offer readers a chance to consider: 1) what their own baptism tells them about who they are and how God sees them; 2) who Jesus is and what following him demands; 3) the transforming grace God offers us; and 4) how this journey with Jesus leads us to a life that is meaningful and amazing.

This four-session study is ideal for discussion groups, such as Sunday school classes and other small groups. Before the first session, each participant will need a copy of the *The Road to Amazing* participant book and should read the Introduction, How to Use This Book, and Chapter 1: Baptism: The Journey Begins. Because not all participants will have an opportunity to read the corresponding chapters in preparation for each session, it will be important for you as the leader to summarize as you move through the discussion, using the helps included in this guide. This will allow everyone to participate fully.

ABOUT THE PARTICIPANT BOOK

This study has been created especially for busy people with many demands on their time. The chapters in the participant book are short and readable, with highlighted subtitles for a quick summary of topics. At the end of each chapter, readers will find a Reflect section to record their thoughts in response to specific questions. Drawing on the imagery of a traveler on a road trip, they will be guided by the following:

 Historical Marker

Historical markers are plaques or signs found in particular locations that commemorate events or persons of historic interest. For our purposes, we will use the term *historical marker* to indicate the study of Holy Scripture. The Bible is full of places, events, and people who have shaped our understanding of God for thousands of years. It's the starting place on the road to amazing!

Each chapter is based on a passage of Scripture, which is printed at the beginning of the chapter. The Historical Marker section invites group members to reflect further on the Scripture passage.

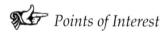 *Points of Interest*

A *point of interest* is a term used to describe interesting and useful locations on maps. It may include geographical landmarks as well as places providing lodging, food, gas stations, or entertainment. This section invites group members to reflect on the insights they gained from each section of the chapter and to note specific points that are significant for them. Surely there are many points of interest along the road to amazing!

 Souvenir

A road trip would be incomplete without a souvenir! Souvenirs are items we keep as reminders of particular events, places, and people. This section invites group members to share what is most memorable about the chapter. Was it a passage of Scripture, a story, or a statement? This is an opportunity to write down the main take-away from the chapter.

Encourage participants to complete each of these three items in the Reflect section of their books, explaining that this will prepare them for the group discussion.

ABOUT THIS LEADER GUIDE

This leader guide is designed to assist you in expedient planning for the group sessions. Four session guides are included, each having a suggested format of 45 to 60 minutes. Additional optional activities are provided to extend the time if needed or desired. Feel free to adapt the format and/or select activities as you wish to tailor the material for the needs of your particular group, making the study your own. You are encouraged to review the guide for each session and use the space provided to create your own plan and write notes.

Here is a brief overview of the elements included in the session guide:

Leader Prep (Before the Session)

For your preparation prior to the group session, this section includes a list of materials needed; a summary of the main idea of the session; the session goals; a biblical foundation or focus Scripture(s), along with brief commentary about the passage(s); and additional Scriptures that give further insights and support to the biblical themes of the session.

Group Session Guide

Welcome/Opening Prayer (5 minutes)

Welcome participants and have everyone introduce themselves if there are newcomers present. Offer a prayer of your own, or use the one provided. You also may wish to invite a group member to pray. Prayer requests may be shared at this time or at the end of the session.

Opening Activity (5 minutes)

Begin the session with an icebreaker introduction to the discussion—a question to put the group at ease and get the conversation going.

Reflect (25–40 minutes)

This portion of the session relates to the Reflect section at the end of the chapter. You will want to encourage participants to refer to that section of the book during this time as you cover the Historical Marker, Points of Interest, and Souvenir exercises there.

 Historical Marker (5–10 minutes)

Read the Scripture aloud and offer background information to provide context for the lesson.

 Points of Interest (15–25 minutes)

This section guides you in focusing on the main insights from the chapter. Present the summary of each section of the chapter, reading the material provided or summarizing it in your own words, and then select from the questions provided to lead discussion of the main points. Material for practical application is provided as well.

 Souvenir (5 minutes)

Next, you will invite group members to share their main take-away—what they will remember most from this lesson.

Wrap Up (5 minutes)

Now it's time to look ahead to next week. Introduce the next chapter briefly and allow time for prayer requests and other announcements.

Closing Prayer (5 minutes)

Conclude the session with prayer. Offer an original prayer, praying specifically for any prayer requests, or pray the prayer provided. You also may invite one of the group members to pray or ask the group to pray the Lord's Prayer together (Matthew 6:9-13).

Extra Material for an Extended Session

Each session guide is followed by additional activities and discussion questions to give you more options in designing the session. This additional material can be used to extend discussion by 15 to 30 minutes. It also serves as a quick go-to resource if the session is running ahead of schedule and you need to fill more time.

— — — — — — — — — — — — — — —

It is our prayer that this study will bring encouragement and inspiration to all who journey on the road to amazing. May God bless you as you lead others to deeper faith in our Lord and Savior, Jesus Christ.

TIPS FOR FACILITATING A SMALL GROUP

- As you prepare for each session, pray for God's guidance. Pray for the participants by name—that each will receive from the study a message to deepen her or his faith as a follower of Jesus.
- Arrive at your meeting place several minutes early to prepare the room. If necessary, rearrange the chairs so participants will be comfortable and able to see each other during the discussion. Small touches such as beverages, refreshments, mints, tissue boxes, and so forth can help create an atmosphere of hospitality and welcome. Your enthusiasm for the opportunity to come together for fellowship and study will set the tone for a positive experience!
- Welcome participants as they arrive. Introduce newcomers and help them get acquainted with others.

- If appropriate, pass around pen and paper in your first session for participants to record their contact information. Seek permission of the group to send a weekly e-mail reminder about the upcoming session, as well as prayer requests that have been shared.
- Ask participants to bring their Bibles to each session. If possible, provide extra Bibles to share with those who did not bring them.
- Make sure everyone has a copy of the book and a pen or pencil.
- Start the session on time.
- As a part of either the opening or closing prayers, invite participants to share prayer requests.
- Throughout the session, include others by inviting them to read Scripture or sections of the chapter, lead in prayer, and so forth. You can simply ask: "Would someone please read/pray?"
- Establish a climate of mutual respect and acceptance that allows each person to share honestly.
- Model openness for sharing by being willing to respond to questions first if no one else does.
- Give gentle reminders regarding time, the amount of material left to cover, and so forth to keep the conversation going forward and to discourage one person from dominating the discussion.
- Encourage everyone's participation by offering positive affirmations for responses and asking further questions to help deepen the discussion.
- At the end of the session, invite participants to the next session by noting the next chapter title.
- End the session with prayer—and end on time! Express gratitude for everyone's attendance and participation in the discussion.

BACKGROUND ON THE GOSPEL OF LUKE

Luke, who also is the author of the Book of Acts, writes his two-volume set (Luke and Acts) to a "most excellent Theophilus," whom some speculate was a Roman official. The name *Theophilus* also means "friend of God." Most scholars date Luke somewhere around the year 80 C.E. or later, which would have been after the fall of Jerusalem, when Christianity was spreading throughout the Roman world. Luke records a story of the birth of Jesus (as does Matthew) and includes the only story in the Gospels about Jesus as a child (when he was twelve and found in the Temple). In fact, while Luke follows the basic outline of Mark and Matthew, a little more than one-third of the Gospel is unique to Luke. Two of the stories chosen for *The Road to Amazing*, the story of Zacchaeus and the road to Emmaus, are found only in Luke.

Luke's purpose in writing is to give "an orderly account" (Luke 1:3) of the events surrounding the life of

Jesus. Luke's Gospel is the longest of the four, giving him time to give an exhaustive account of Jesus and his place as the centerpiece of God's salvation history. One of the most important questions he seeks to answer—"Who is Jesus?"—is the focus of Chapter 2 in our study.

There are a number of key themes to be aware of as you read Luke. First of all, Luke emphasizes the inclusive nature of God's love. God's offer of salvation extends beyond the boundaries of the Jewish community into the Gentile world. The love of Jesus is for all people, including sinners, tax collectors, and other outcasts. Luke also lifts up the role and place of women. This is a radical concept in light of how women were treated in biblical times—something we may not at first recognize. Luke demonstrates that Jesus has a special concern for the poor and harsh words for the wealthy. Mary's song in Luke 1:46-55 goes so far as to say that God "has filled the hungry with good things, and sent the rich away empty" (v. 53). The Gospel also has many stories of table fellowship, perhaps not surprising for one who found the presence of Jesus made real "in the breaking of the bread" (Luke 24:35).

Session 1

BAPTISM

The Journey Begins

Leader Prep

Materials Needed

- *The Road to Amazing* books and Bibles
- Pens and pencils
- Board and chalk or chart paper and marker
- Copy of the baptismal covenant service or vows of your denomination (optional activity)

Main Idea

Baptism becomes the primary source of identity for Christians. As we begin an amazing journey with Jesus, baptism tells us who we are as God's children, what God has done for us through forgiveness, and how God's Spirit empowers us for living.

Session Goals

This session is intended to help participants:

- Understand the importance of Jesus' baptism and our baptism.
- Recognize God's claim on our lives through baptism.
- Acknowledge God's forgiving action through baptism.
- Consider what it means to live life trusting God and seeking God's will for our lives.

Biblical Foundation

[21] *Now when all the people were baptized, and when Jesus also had been baptized and was praying, the heaven was opened,* [22] *and the Holy Spirit descended upon him in bodily form like a dove. And a voice came from heaven, "You are my Son, the Beloved; with you I am well pleased."*

(Luke 3:21-22)

The baptism of Jesus appears to initiate his public ministry. Was he aware of his identity before this event? The answer to this question has been debated through the centuries. It may be interesting to compare and contrast the various Gospel writers' versions of his baptism:

- In Matthew's Gospel, we see that John the Baptist is reluctant to baptize Jesus, saying that he should be baptized by Jesus instead. Jesus encourages John to let it be so for now in order to fulfill righteousness (Matthew 3:13-17).

- In Mark's Gospel, we have the straightforward story of Jesus being baptized by John without any conversation between the two (Mark 1:9-11).
- In Luke's Gospel, we find a brief statement telling us simply that Jesus was baptized and the Spirit descended on him like a dove. Interestingly, we find this statement after we are told that John the Baptist has been arrested, and so only by implication can we assume he was baptized by John (Luke 3:21-22).
- In John's Gospel, John the Baptist is across the Jordan from where he was baptizing when he is questioned about who he is, and he acknowledges that the Messiah is present among them. The next day he identifies Jesus as the Lamb of God, saying that he saw the Spirit descending like a dove on Jesus. However, the text does not directly state that Jesus is baptized (John 1:29-34).

Each of the Gospels talks about the Spirit descending on Jesus as a dove during this baptism event, giving him an identity: God's Son.

In the Book of Acts, also written by Luke, baptism plays a central role in the life of the early church. On the Day of Pentecost, when the disciples are filled with the Holy Spirit, Peter preaches and the crowd wants to know what they must do to be saved. Peter's response, is, "Repent, and be baptized every one of you in the name of Jesus Christ so that your sins may be forgiven; and you will receive the gift of the Holy Spirit" (Acts 2:38). Three thousand people respond and are baptized into this new church community.

Later in the Book of Acts, Luke tells the baptism stories of the Ethiopian eunuch (Acts 8:26-40), Paul (Acts 9:18), Gentiles (Acts 10:47-48), Lydia and her household (Acts 16:15), a jailer and his household (Acts 16:33), Crispus and many of the Corinthians (Acts 18:8), and disciples in Ephesus (Acts 19:1-7). Clearly baptism was a way of initiating new believers into the community of faith. It was an outward act giving these new believers an identity as part of the community of God's people. Baptism reminded them that their sins had been forgiven and called them forth to lead a new life, led by the Spirit of the living God.

Baptism is the beginning point on the road to amazing.

Additional Scriptures

[18]And Jesus came and said to them, "All authority in heaven and on earth has been given to me. [19]Go therefore and make disciples of all nations, baptizing them in the name of the Father and of the Son and of the Holy Spirit, [20]and teaching them to obey everything that I have commanded you. And remember, I am with you always, to the end of the age."

(Matthew 28:18-19)

[1]I therefore, the prisoner in the Lord, beg you to lead a life worthy of the calling to which you have been called, [2]with all humility and gentleness, with patience, bearing with one another in love, [3]making every effort to maintain the unity of the Spirit in the bond of peace. [4]There is one body and one Spirit, just as you were called to the one hope of your calling, [5]one Lord, one faith, one baptism, [6]one God and Father of all, who is above all and through all and in all.

(Ephesians 4:1-6)

18

Session Guide

Welcome/Opening Prayer (5 minutes)

Welcome participants and make introductions, if necessary. You may wish to begin with prayer requests to include in the opening prayer, or you may save these for the closing prayer time. Note that today's session is the first of a four-part series and make sure everyone has a copy of *The Road to Amazing* book. If appropriate, pass around a sign-up sheet to gather contact information. Seek permission of the group to set up a group e-mail so that you can send a weekly reminder about the chapter you will be studying, as well as prayer requests.

Now lead the group in an opening prayer, or ask a participant to pray. You may use your own prayer or the one below:

O God, you are amazing, and you call us to walk with you on a road to amazing. Help us to know you. Help us to know ourselves. We are your beloved children. We belong to you, for you have called us by name. Thank you for loving us, forgiving us, and setting us free to follow you. Send your Spirit upon us, gathered here out of love for you. May your Spirit guide us in the way you would have us go. In Jesus' name. Amen.

Opening Activity (5 minutes)

To introduce the study, read or ask a participant to read the Introduction in *The Road to Amazing* (pages 11–12).

Reflect (25–40 minutes)

As you begin the Reflect section, review and explain the terms Historical Marker, Points of Interest, and Souvenir (see pages 14–15 in "How to Use This Book"). You will want to encourage participants to refer to the Reflect section at the end of the chapter during this time.

 *Historical Marker (5–10 minutes)*

Ask different participants to read the four accounts of Jesus' baptism.

Then Jesus came from Galilee to John at the Jordan, to be baptized by him. John would have prevented him, saying, "I need to be baptized by you, and do you come to me?" But Jesus answered him, "Let it be so now; for it is proper for us in this way to fulfill all righteousness." Then he consented. And when Jesus had been baptized, just as he came up from the water, suddenly the heavens were opened to him and he saw the Spirit of God descending like a dove and alighting on him. And a voice from heaven said, "This is my Son, the Beloved, with whom I am well pleased."
(Matthew 3:13-17)

In those days Jesus came from Nazareth of Galilee and was baptized by John in the Jordan. And just as he was coming up out of the water, he saw the heavens torn apart and the Spirit descending like a dove on him. And a voice came from heaven, "You are my Son, the Beloved; with you I am well pleased."
(Mark 1:9-11)

Now when all the people were baptized, and when Jesus also had been baptized and was praying, the heaven was opened, and the Holy Spirit descended upon him in bodily form like a dove. And a voice came from heaven, "You are my Son, the Beloved; with you I am well pleased."
(Luke 3:21-22)

The next day he saw Jesus coming toward him and declared, "Here is the Lamb of God who takes away the sin of the world! This is he of whom I said, 'After me comes a man who ranks ahead of me because he was before me.' I myself did not know him; but I came baptizing with water for this reason, that he might be revealed to Israel." And John testified, "I saw the Spirit descending from heaven like a dove, and it remained on him. I myself did not know him, but the one who sent me to baptize with water said to me, 'He on whom you see the Spirit descend and remain is the one who baptizes with the Holy Spirit.' And I myself have seen and have testified that this is the Son of God."

(John 1:29-34)

Ask participants to name the similarities and differences in the accounts as you list them on a board or chart paper. Ask:

Is there an account of Jesus' baptism that is especially meaningful to you? Why?

 *Points of Interest (15–25 minutes)*

Summarize each of the sections below, pausing after each summary to ask group members to share the insights they listed in their books. Discuss why the insights were significant to them, and ask how these insights will be applied in daily living.

- *Why Is Baptism Important?*

Summary: Established in Scripture and lived out in tradition, the sacrament of baptism marks initiation, or entry, into the household of faith at whatever age it is received. It is the beginning of an amazing journey.

21

Other notes:

Discuss the following:

- What insights did you record in your books?
- Why were these insights significant to you?
- How can you apply these insights in your daily living?

- *Claimed by God*

Summary: In the waters of baptism, we receive the gift that God has claimed us as God's children. You are a child of God. This is a reminder of God's prevenient grace, the grace that precedes your awareness or response. It is God initiating a relationship with you. In baptism, the emphasis is not on the worthiness of the believer, but on the goodness of God.

Other notes:

Discuss the following:

- What insights did you record in your books?
- Why were these insights significant to you?
- How can you apply these insights in your daily living?

- *Forgiven*

Summary: We forgive because we have been forgiven. Our baptism is a powerful reminder of this truth. Every time we remember our baptism, we are claiming this truth: our sins have been forgiven!

Other notes:

Discuss the following:

- What insights did you record in your books?
- Why were these insights significant to you?
- How can you apply these insights in your daily living?

- *Spirit-led*

Summary: In baptism we are given an identity as children of God who have been forgiven by God. Our baptism also helps us recognize that our lives are being led by the Holy Spirit.

Other notes:

Discuss the following:

- What insights did you record in your books?
- Why were these insights significant to you?
- How can you apply these insights in your daily living?

Souvenir (5 minutes)

Invite participants to share their answers to the question *What "souvenir" will you take with you as a remembrance of this chapter?* and tell why this was especially meaningful to them. Be prepared to share your own answer first if necessary.

Wrap Up (5 minutes)

Ask participants to turn to Chapter 2: Defining Moments on the Journey (page 41). Say: "Our next session will focus on Luke 9:18-27. I look forward to this time of study and prayer with each of you."

Closing Prayer (5 minutes)

Lead the group in prayer. You may pray the one provided below, offer one of your own, or invite a participant to pray. If prayer requests were shared at the beginning, remind the group to include these in their daily prayer time in the coming week. Or invite prayer requests at this time and include them in the prayer. Another option is to invite everyone to recite the Lord's Prayer (Matthew 6:9-13).

Dear Lord, in baptism you have given us an identity. More important than how much is in our bank accounts, what we do for a living, where we live, our race, or any other fact about our lives, this one fact we cling to: we are yours. Thank you for accepting us, forgiving us, and leading us into a new way of life. Help us day by day to live like your children. Lord, there are so many people who have had their identity stolen by the world. Use us to show others their true identity. Through our actions, help us to show the love of Christ to everyone we meet. In Jesus' name. Amen.

Extra Material for an Extended Session

Extra Activities

- Ask participants to describe a time when they had a strong sense of belonging and felt welcomed and accepted.
- Review together the baptismal covenant, or vows, made at baptism in your denomination.
- Ask participants to look up and read Scriptures included in the Additional Scriptures section. You may wish to write the list of Scriptures on a chalkboard or on individual pieces of paper to distribute.

Extra Discussion Questions

- Have you been baptized? What do you know/remember about the event? What is special to you about those memories?
- What new insights about baptism did you receive from this study? How will this impact your faith journey?

Notes for the Session

Session 2

DEFINING MOMENTS ON THE JOURNEY

Leader Prep

Materials Needed

- *The Road to Amazing* books and Bibles
- Pens and pencils
- "A Covenant Prayer in the Wesleyan Tradition," see *The Road to Amazing*, page 47 (optional activity)

Main Idea

Along the road, we are confronted with a question: Who is Jesus? We must answer the question for ourselves, consider the cost of following, and make a daily decision to serve Christ.

Session Goals

This session is intended to help participants:

- Recognize Jesus' message of self-denial and losing one's life for his sake as countercultural.
- Consider the seriousness of following Jesus and its possible implications.
- Reflect on how defining moments are played out in our daily lives.
- Discern what Christ may be calling us to do.

Biblical Foundation

18Once when Jesus was praying alone, with only the disciples near him, he asked them, "Who do the crowds say that I am?" 19They answered, "John the Baptist; but others, Elijah; and still others, that one of the ancient prophets has arisen." 20He said to them, "But who do you say that I am?" Peter answered, "The Messiah of God."

21He sternly ordered and commanded them not to tell anyone, 22saying, "The Son of Man must undergo great suffering, and be rejected by the elders, chief priests, and scribes, and be killed, and on the third day be raised."

23Then he said to them all, "If any want to become my followers, let them deny themselves and take up their cross daily and follow me. 24For those who want to save their life will lose it, and those who lose their life for my sake will save it. 25What does it profit them if they gain the whole world, but lose or forfeit themselves? 26Those who are ashamed of me and of my words, of them the Son of Man will be ashamed when he comes in his glory and the glory of the Father and of the holy angels. 27But truly I tell you, there are some standing here who will not taste death before they see the kingdom of God."

(Luke 9:18-27)

Luke 9:18-27 is one of the most pivotal passages in Luke's Gospel. The disciples, and all who read this text, are confronted with an important question. After asking the disciples what the crowds are saying about him, Jesus asks, "But who do you say that I am" (Luke 9:20a). It is a question every Christian must answer along the journey of faith. Is Jesus a good man? A prophet? A religious zealot? A political revolutionary? A miracle worker?

Peter answers Jesus quickly and simply: "The Messiah of God" (Luke 9:20b). *Messiah* is a term that means "anointed one" or "Christ." For centuries the Hebrew people had awaited a Messiah who would restore the kingdom of Israel. The expectation was that the Messiah would be more of a political or military leader. Did Jesus fit the expectation?

Once Peter answers Jesus, the disciples are confronted with what following this Messiah means. They must put their agendas aside, take up their cross daily, and follow Jesus. As we see in Chapter 2 of *The Road to Amazing*, Luke's version of this story adds a word not contained in Mark's and Matthew's versions: *daily*. Why is this? When Luke writes his Gospel, it has now been some fifty years since the crucifixion and resurrection of Jesus. Earlier writings contain an expectation that Jesus will return any day. Luke's reality is that he has not yet returned, and so people must figure out not only how to be ready to die for Jesus but also how to be ready to live for Jesus on a daily basis. This is at least one thought as to why Luke added this word.

Jesus turns the world's order of priorities upside down with his statement about losing your life in order to save it. Much of the world then—as now—would say, *If you want to save your life, then play it safe*. Jesus presents a new understanding of what living life is all about. In order to fully experience life, you must learn how to give your life away.

Additional Scriptures

²¹From that time on, Jesus began to show his disciples that he must go to Jerusalem and undergo great suffering at the hands of the elders and chief priests and scribes, and be killed, and on the third day be raised. ²²And Peter took him aside and began to rebuke him, saying, "God forbid it, Lord! This must never happen to you." ²³But he turned and said to Peter, "Get behind me, Satan! You are a stumbling block to me; for you are setting your mind not on divine things but on human things."

²⁴Then Jesus told his disciples, "If any want to become my followers, let them deny themselves and take up their cross and follow me. ²⁵For those who want to save their life will lose it, and those who lose their life for my sake will find it. ²⁶For what will it profit them if they gain the whole world but forfeit their life? Or what will they give in return for their life?"

(Matthew 16:21-26)

⁷Yet whatever gains I had, these I have come to regard as loss because of Christ. ⁸More than that, I regard everything as loss because of the surpassing value of knowing Christ Jesus my Lord. For his sake I have suffered the loss of all things, and I regard them as rubbish, in order that I may gain Christ ⁹and be found in him, not having a righteousness of my own that comes from the law, but one that comes through faith in Christ, the righteousness from God based on faith. ¹⁰I want to know Christ and the power of his resurrection and the sharing of his sufferings by becoming like him in his death.

(Philippians 3:7-10)

Do your best to present yourself to God as one approved by him, a worker who has no need to be ashamed, rightly explaining the word of truth.

(2 Timothy 2:15)

[17]*As he was setting out on a journey, a man ran up and knelt before him, and asked him, "Good Teacher, what must I do to inherit eternal life?"* [18]*Jesus said to him, "Why do you call me good? No one is good but God alone.* [19]*You know the commandments: 'You shall not murder; You shall not commit adultery; You shall not steal; You shall not bear false witness; You shall not defraud; Honor your father and mother.'"* [20]*He said to him, "Teacher, I have kept all these since my youth."* [21]*Jesus, looking at him, loved him and said, "You lack one thing; go, sell what you own, and give the money to the poor, and you will have treasure in heaven; then come, follow me."* [22]*When he heard this, he was shocked and went away grieving, for he had many possessions.*

[23]*Then Jesus looked around and said to his disciples, "How hard it will be for those who have wealth to enter the kingdom of God!"* [24]*And the disciples were perplexed at these words. But Jesus said to them again, "Children, how hard it is to enter the kingdom of God!* [25]*It is easier for a camel to go through the eye of a needle than for someone who is rich to enter the kingdom of God."* [26]*They were greatly astounded and said to one another, "Then who can be saved?"* [27]*Jesus looked at them and said, "For mortals it is impossible, but not for God; for God all things are possible."*

(Mark 10:17-27)

Session Guide

Welcome/Opening Prayer (5 minutes)

Welcome participants and make introductions, if necessary. You may wish to begin with prayer requests to include in the opening prayer, or you may save these for the closing prayer time.

Now lead the group in an opening prayer, or ask a participant to pray. You may use your own prayer or the one below:

O God, you are the Creator and Source of all life. You so loved the world that you sent your Son Jesus to offer us life, now and forever. Thank you for the gift of Jesus. Help us to truly turn over our lives to him. May we put aside our self-interest, and focus on what you would have us do. Open our minds that we may consider the cost of following you. Give to each of us a new spiritual insight about our own faith in you. In Jesus' name. Amen.

Opening Activity (5 minutes)

Ask participants to share stories of people they have known who exemplified what it meant to "deny yourself and take up your cross daily" to follow Jesus.

Reflect (25–40 minutes)

You will want to encourage participants to refer to the Reflect section at the end of the chapter during this time.

 Historical Marker (5–10 minutes)

Read or ask a group member to read Luke 9:18-27, followed by the contextual background of this Scripture reading found on pages 60–61 of *The Road to Amazing*. You may wish to share more background about this particular Scripture (see "Biblical Foundation," pages 28–30 in this Leader Guide.)

Ask group members to share their responses to the question in this section:

- How would you answer Jesus' question, "Who do you say that I am?"

 *Points of Interest (15–25 minutes)*

Summarize each of the sections below, pausing after each summary to ask group members to share the insights they listed in their books. Discuss why the insights were significant to them, and ask how these insights will be applied in daily living.

- *Win by Losing*

Summary: Christians are called to a different way of life than just dividing the world into winners and losers. Christians are called to win by losing.

Other notes:

Discuss the following:

- What insights did you record in your books?
- Why were these insights significant to you?
- How can you apply these insights in your daily living?

- *Deny Yourself*

Summary: Jesus' message to "deny yourself" is so challenging because we have bought into the myth that it's all about us. The message of Jesus is countercultural. It challenges us to a life of self-denial in which we put Christ first.

Other notes:

Discuss the following:

- What insights did you record in your books?
- Why were these insights significant to you?
- How can you apply these insights in your daily living?

- *Take Up Your Cross*

Summary: Jesus also told the disciples to "take up your cross daily and follow me." The word *cross* in the Greek could mean, in terms of execution by crucifixion, the capital punishment instrument used by the Romans. He was telling his followers they would need to count the cost of following him and be willing to pay the price. So people of that day thought about the word *cross* in terms of "We all have a cross to bear." If you take up your cross, it may mean death.

Other notes:

Discuss the following:

- What insights did you record in your books?
- Why were these insights significant to you?

- How can you apply these insights in your daily living?

- *Daily*

Summary: The Greek word *stauros* is translated as "cross." It also means "stake," such as a stake that is stuck in the ground to secure a tent or tether an animal.[1] So Jesus' statement to the disciples could also mean to pull up the stake to which you are tethered, so you can move out of your comfort zone. Pull up your stake, lose your security, and follow Jesus where it is risky. Jesus calls us to this task daily.[2]

Other notes:

Discuss the following:

- What insights did you record in your books?
- Why were these insights significant to you?
- How can you apply these insights in your daily living?

- *What Is Christ Calling You to Do?*

Summary: Christ calls all of us to a life of self-denial. It's countercultural; not what our society preaches. Self-denial and taking up your cross to go where he leads you: what would that mean for you in your life?

Other notes:

Discuss the following:

- What insights did you record in your books?
- Why were these insights significant to you?
- How can you apply these insights in your daily living?

 Souvenir (5 minutes)

Invite participants to share their answers to the question *What "souvenir" will you take with you as a remembrance of this chapter?* and tell why this was especially meaningful to them. Be prepared to share your own answer first if necessary.

Wrap Up (5 minutes)

Ask participants to turn to Chapter 3: Transforming Journey (page 63). Note the title and the Reflect section for the next session. Say: "Our next session will focus on Luke 19:1-10. I look forward to this time of study and prayer with each of you."

Closing Prayer (5 minutes)

Lead the group in prayer. You may pray the one provided below, offer one of your own, or invite a participant to pray. If prayer requests were shared at the beginning, remind the group to include these in their daily prayer time in the coming week. Or invite prayer requests at this time and include them in the prayer. Another option is to invite everyone to recite the Lord's Prayer (Matthew 6:9-13).

Gracious and loving God, we are challenged by your Word. It's not easy for us to think about stepping out of control and giving up ourselves, our control, and our desire to set our own path. This day we recommit ourselves to you. We invite you into our hearts anew this day and ask that you take our lives. Use them as you will and forgive us. We've tried to set the agenda instead of following your agenda. We pray that this would be a day of new beginnings, and we give ourselves fully to you and surrender. In Jesus' name. Amen.

Extra Material for an Extended Session

Extra Activities

- Review "A Covenant Prayer in the Wesleyan Tradition" (see *The Road to Amazing*, page 47). Ask participants to describe the level of commitment needed to pray this prayer. You may wish to pray it together as you close your session.
- Ask participants to look up and read Scriptures from the Additional Scriptures section. You may wish to write the list of Scriptures on a chalkboard or on individual pieces of paper to distribute.

Extra Discussion Questions

- How can we serve Christ daily in our work, in our families, in our leisure, and in our communities?
- As you think of the challenges in your own particular community, where might Christ be calling you to "deny yourself" and follow him by serving others?

Notes for the Session

TRANSFORMING JOURNEY

Leader Prep

Materials Needed

- *The Road to Amazing* books and Bibles
- Pens and pencils

Main Idea

As Zacchaeus found out, when we encounter Jesus along the journey, our lives are never the same.

Session Goals

This session is intended to help participants:

- Reflect on the ways we measure success in life.
- Consider the importance of truth-telling in keeping us honest about our values.

- Recognize the ways God works in our lives to bring about salvation and transformation.

Biblical Foundation

¹*[Jesus] entered Jericho and was passing through it.* ²*A man was there named Zacchaeus; he was a chief tax collector and was rich.* ³*He was trying to see who Jesus was, but on account of the crowd he could not, because he was short in stature.* ⁴*So he ran ahead and climbed a sycamore tree to see him, because he was going to pass that way.* ⁵*When Jesus came to the place, he looked up and said to him, "Zacchaeus, hurry and come down; for I must stay at your house today."* ⁶*So he hurried down and was happy to welcome him.* ⁷*All who saw it began to grumble and said, "He has gone to be the guest of one who is a sinner."* ⁸*Zacchaeus stood there and said to the Lord, "Look, half of my possessions, Lord, I will give to the poor; and if I have defrauded anyone of anything, I will pay back four times as much."* ⁹*Then Jesus said to him, "Today salvation has come to this house, because he too is a son of Abraham.* ¹⁰*For the Son of Man came to seek out and to save the lost."*

(Luke 19:1-10)

Luke is the only Gospel that tells the story of Zacchaeus the tax collector and the transformation that occurs in his life as he encounters Jesus. The story takes place in the city of Jericho, the same city talked about in the Book of Joshua, in which Joshua fought the battle of Jericho (Joshua 5:13–6:27). Jesus, whose name is the Greek form of the Hebrew name Joshua, has come to Jericho to tear down the walls built up in the life of Zacchaeus. Luke tells us that Zacchaeus was a chief tax collector and was rich. Tax collectors worked for the Romans, collecting taxes from their own people. Most were known to be corrupt, collecting enough to satisfy the Romans while skimming off the top to fulfill a desire for more wealth. We don't know for sure that Zacchaeus is corrupt until after his meeting with Jesus, when he basically admits it by offering to repay those he has cheated. The law required that the offending party pay back twice as much as was originally taken, but Zacchaeus offers to repay it fourfold, going far beyond what was required.

Another part of this story that is interesting to explore is the reaction of the crowd outside the home of Zacchaeus. Jesus has gone to be the guest of someone who is a sinner, and they grumble about it. In biblical times, as today, we like it when Jesus loves and pays attention to people who are obviously good people and deserve to be in his company, but it flies all over us when Jesus offers grace and love to people we believe are not worthy of it. The truth is none of us are worthy of his love and grace, but Jesus offers it anyway.

This passage is a prime example of Luke's desire for all to understand that the love of Jesus is more expansive than the boundaries we set. Jesus has come to seek and to save the lost, and we must follow his lead on the road to amazing.

Additional Scriptures

Do not be conformed to this world, but be transformed by the renewing of your minds, so that you may discern what is the will of God—what is good and acceptable and perfect.

(Romans 12:2)

So if anyone is in Christ, there is a new creation: everything old has passed away; see, everything has become new!

(2 Corinthians 5:17)

[22]*You were taught to put away your former way of life, your old self, corrupt and deluded by its lusts,* [23]*and to be renewed in the spirit of your minds,* [24]*and to clothe yourselves with the new self, created according to the likeness of God in true righteousness and holiness.*

(Ephesians 4:22-24)

A new heart I will give you, and a new spirit I will put within you; and I will remove from your body the heart of stone and give you a heart of flesh.

(Ezekiel 36:26)

Create in me a clean heart, O God,
and put a new and right spirit within me.
(Psalm 51:10)

[11:27]But the thing that David had done displeased the LORD, [12:1]and the LORD sent Nathan to David. He came to him, and said to him, "There were two men in a certain city, the one rich and the other poor. [2]The rich man had very many flocks and herds; [3]but the poor man had nothing but one little ewe lamb, which he had bought. He brought it up, and it grew up with him and with his children; it used to eat of his meagre fare, and drink from his cup, and lie in his bosom, and it was like a daughter to him. [4]Now there came a traveler to the rich man, and he was loath to take one of his own flock or herd to prepare for the wayfarer who had come to him, but he took the poor man's lamb, and prepared that for the guest who had come to him." [5]Then David's anger was greatly kindled against the man. He said to Nathan, "As the LORD lives, the man who has done this deserves to die; [6]he shall restore the lamb fourfold, because he did this thing, and because he had no pity."

[7]Nathan said to David, "You are the man!"

(2 Samuel 11:27b–12:7a)

Session Guide

Welcome/Opening Prayer (5 minutes)

Welcome participants. You may wish to begin with prayer requests to include in the opening prayer, or you may save these for the closing prayer time.

Now lead the group in an opening prayer, or ask a participant to pray. You may use your own prayer or the one below:

Gracious and loving God, thank you for this day of life. What a gift you have given us! As we study your Word today, send your Spirit to transform our hearts. All of us stand in need of your grace. Many of us find ourselves lost, and sometimes we don't even know it. But you seek us out, and want to come to our house today. Speak to us that we may hear, and act upon what we hear. Your gift of salvation is offered to each of us and to all the world. Help us to accept this gift. In Jesus' name. Amen.

Opening Activity (5 minutes)

Ask participants to share a word, phrase, or image to describe the word *transformation*.

Reflect (25–40 minutes)

You will want to encourage participants to refer to the Reflect section at the end of the chapter during this time.

 Historical Marker (10 minutes)

Read or ask a group member to read Luke 19:1-10, followed by the contextual background of this Scripture reading found on pages 81–82 of *The Road to Amazing*. You may wish to share more background about this particular Scripture (see "Biblical Foundation," pages 40–41 of this Leader guide.)

Ask group members to share their responses to the question in this section:

- If Jesus came to your house, in what ways might you expect your life to be transformed?

 *Points of Interest (15–25 minutes)*

Summarize each of the sections below, pausing after each summary to ask group members to share the insights they listed in their books. Discuss why the insights were significant to them, and ask how these insights will be applied in daily living.

- *Measurements*

Summary: For Zacchaeus, measuring a life seemed to be about wealth and position. Jesus challenged him, as he challenges us today, to look at the ways we measure success for ourselves and others.

Other notes:

Discuss the following:

- What insights did you record in your books?
- Why were these insights significant to you?
- How can you apply these insights in your daily living?

- *Lost*

Summary: We may not feel lost, but sometimes we pause to look up, and we realize we're not living life the way God would have us live it. Somewhere along the way Zacchaeus realized he was lost; despite his wealth, his life was not abundant. Sometimes along the way it happens to us too. Thank God that Jesus loves lost people!

Other notes:

Discuss the following:

- What insights did you record in your books?
- Why were these insights significant to you?
- How can you apply these insights in your daily living?

- *Truth*

Summary: Zacchaeus found that he had someone in Jesus who was willing to tell him the truth. No doubt as they shared a meal together in Zacchaeus's home, Jesus spoke the truth in love. Jesus knows who you are and challenges you to get truthful about who you are. Knowing that you are loved by God, in spite of what you have done, you have an opportunity to move forward in your life in a positive direction.

Other notes:

Discuss the following:

- What insights did you record in your book?
- Why were these insights significant to you?
- How can you apply these insights in your daily living?

- *Salvation*

Summary: Salvation is best understood as a process, rather than a one-time event. The day Jesus came to the home of Zacchaeus was only the beginning of the story. Zacchaeus met the Truth and the Truth set him free. He found out the truth about who he was—that he was a child of God. That truth gives us value and a means by which to measure our lives.

Other notes:

Discuss the following:

- What insights did you record in your book?
- Why were these insights significant to you?
- How can you apply these insights in your daily living?

- *Transformation*

Summary: Transformation may be experienced in a dramatic way, but some of us don't really feel any different than we always have. As we begin to examine our lives, however, we realize that we have changed—following

Jesus has shifted our priorities, our actions, and our attitudes. Theologians call this *sanctification*—the grace that God works in our lives from the time of our acceptance of a relationship with Jesus on through the rest of our lives. God's sanctifying grace shapes and molds us, moving us ever closer to a life aligned with the love of Christ.

Other notes:

Discuss the following:

- What insights did you record in your books?
- Why were these insights significant to you?
- How can you apply these insights in your daily living?

 *Souvenir (5 minutes)*

Invite participants to share their answers to the question *What "souvenir" will you take with you as a remembrance of this chapter?* and tell why this was especially meaningful to them. Be prepared to share your own answer first if necessary.

Wrap Up (5 minutes)

Ask participants to turn to Chapter 4: The Road to Amazing (page 85). Say: "Our next session will focus on Luke 24:13-35. I look forward to this time of study and prayer with each of you."

Closing Prayer (5 minutes)

Lead the group in prayer. You may pray the one provided below, offer one of your own, or invite a participant to pray. If prayer requests were shared at the beginning, remind the group to include these in their daily prayer time in the coming week. Or invite prayer requests at this time and include them in the prayer. Another option is to invite everyone to recite the Lord's Prayer (Matthew 6:9-13).

Gracious God, some of us are so busy and hurried, struggling trying to find balance in life, and sometimes you send us these lessons in your Word that just cut right through it all to remind us about what really matters. We're thankful, Lord, that you came to seek and to save lost people like us, and we pray that salvation would come to all of our houses today. We pray that we may understand what really matters in life as you tell us the truth about who we are as your beloved children. Bless everyone here, and help us to learn how to measure the things that matter. In Jesus' name. Amen.

Extra Material for an Extended Session

Extra Activities

- Reread Luke 19:1-10. Ask participants: Who do you most identify with in this story—Zacchaeus or the people of Jericho? Why?
- Ask participants to look up and read Scriptures from the Additional Scriptures section. You may wish to list the Scriptures on a chalkboard or on individual pieces of paper to distribute.

Extra Discussion Questions

- In the culture of Jesus' day, what were the important measurements by which people measured themselves? How are these measurements the same or different today?
- In biblical times, tax collectors, prostitutes, adulterers, Samaritans, Gentiles, and others were looked down upon as outcasts. Who would we identify as outcasts today? How would Jesus want us to treat them?

Notes for the Session

Session 4

THE ROAD TO AMAZING

Leader Prep

Materials Needed

- *The Road to Amazing* books and Bibles
- Pens and pencils

Main Idea

Join the disciples who walked the road to Emmaus with the risen Christ, and discover how Jesus continually "shows up" and is present in every journey.

Session Goals

This session is intended to help participants:

- Recognize the ways God walks beside us in times of tribulation.

- Claim the promise of new life and God's love, from which we can never be separated.

Biblical Foundation

[13]*Now on that same day two of them were going to a village called Emmaus, about seven miles from Jerusalem,* [14]*and talking with each other about all these things that had happened.* [15]*While they were talking and discussing, Jesus himself came near and went with them,* [16]*but their eyes were kept from recognizing him.* [17]*And he said to them, "What are you discussing with each other while you walk along?" They stood still, looking sad.* [18]*Then one of them, whose name was Cleopas, answered him, "Are you the only stranger in Jerusalem who does not know the things that have taken place there in these days?"* [19]*He asked them, "What things?" They replied, "The things about Jesus of Nazareth, who was a prophet mighty in deed and word before God and all the people,* [20]*and how our chief priests and leaders handed him over to be condemned to death and crucified him.* [21]*But we had hoped that he was the one to redeem Israel. Yes, and besides all this, it is now the third day since these things took place.* [22]*Moreover, some women of our group astounded us. They were at the tomb early this morning,* [23]*and when they did not find his body there, they came back and told us that they had indeed seen a vision of angels who said that he was alive.* [24]*Some of those who were with us went to the tomb and found it just as the women had said; but they did not see him."* [25]*Then he said to them, "Oh, how foolish you are, and how slow of heart to believe all that the prophets have declared!* [26]*Was it not necessary that the Messiah should suffer these things and then enter into his glory?"* [27]*Then beginning with Moses and all the prophets, he interpreted to them the things about himself in all the scriptures.*

[28]*As they came near the village to which they were going, he walked ahead as if he were going on.* [29]*But they urged him strongly,*

saying, "Stay with us, because it is almost evening and the day is now nearly over." So he went in to stay with them. ³⁰When he was at the table with them, he took bread, blessed and broke it, and gave it to them. ³¹Then their eyes were opened, and they recognized him; and he vanished from their sight. ³²They said to each other, "Were not our hearts burning within us while he was talking to us on the road, while he was opening the scriptures to us?" ³³That same hour they got up and returned to Jerusalem; and they found the eleven and their companions gathered together. ³⁴They were saying, "The Lord has risen indeed, and he has appeared to Simon!" ³⁵Then they told what had happened on the road, and how he had been made known to them in the breaking of the bread.

(Luke 24:13-35)

The Road to Emmaus story is found only in the Gospel of Luke, although it likely existed in oral tradition prior to the writing of the Gospel. In fact, Mark's Gospel seems to reference it in Mark 16:12-13, which is a short version of this story (typical of Mark). Cleopas and his unnamed companion are walking to the village of Emmaus, about seven miles from Jerusalem, when a stranger joins them. It was the resurrected Jesus, but their eyes were kept from recognizing him. Did God keep them from recognizing Jesus? Or was this more about the condition they were in, finding themselves downcast in grief?

Jesus listens to their story, and then chides them for their lack of faith. He opens the Scriptures and, beginning with Moses and all the prophets, he interprets the Scriptures for them. For Luke, this is a key theme: Jesus is the culmination and centerpiece of the salvation history that God began among the Hebrew people long ago. In Jesus, the covenant relationship is now fulfilled and expanded to all the world.

At the close of the day, the men near their destination, and Jesus (the stranger) appears to be traveling on. They implore him to stay with them. As they sit down to eat a meal, Jesus takes the bread, blesses it, breaks it, and gives it to them. It is in the breaking of the bread that their eyes are opened and they recognize him. He had been with them all day, but until this moment they did not know who he was. As they run back to tell the others, they reflect on how their hearts burned when he was with them on the road.

How often we look back and see that Jesus was with us all along our journey and we did not realize it! This story lends itself to discussions of the meaning and experience of Communion, as well as the Christian journey itself. Jesus is made real to us as we fellowship with others, journey with others, and serve with others. His presence with us makes our journey amazing!

Additional Scriptures

[10]Jacob left Beer-sheba and went towards Haran. [11]He came to a certain place and stayed there for the night, because the sun had set. Taking one of the stones of the place, he put it under his head and lay down in that place. [12]And he dreamed that there was a ladder set up on the earth, the top of it reaching to heaven; and the angels of God were ascending and descending on it. [13]And the Lord stood beside him and said, "I am the LORD, the God of Abraham your father and the God of Isaac; the land on which you lie I will give to you and to your offspring; [14]and your offspring shall be like the dust of the earth, and you shall spread abroad to the west and to the east and to the north and to the south; and all the families of the earth shall be blessed in you and in your offspring. [15]Know that I am with you and will keep you wherever you go, and will bring you back to this land; for I will not leave you until I have

done what I have promised you." ¹⁶Then Jacob woke from his sleep and said, "Surely the LORD is in this place—and I did not know it!" ¹⁷And he was afraid, and said, "How awesome is this place! This is none other than the house of God, and this is the gate of heaven."

(Genesis 28:10-17)

¹ *O* LORD, *you have searched me and known me.*
² *You know when I sit down and when I rise up;*
  you discern my thoughts from far away.
³ *You search out my path and my lying down,*
  and are acquainted with all my ways.
⁴ *Even before a word is on my tongue,*
  O LORD, *you know it completely.*
⁵ *You hem me in, behind and before,*
  and lay your hand upon me.
⁶ *Such knowledge is too wonderful for me;*
  it is so high that I cannot attain it.

⁷ *Where can I go from your spirit?*
  Or where can I flee from your presence?
⁸ *If I ascend to heaven, you are there;*
  if I make my bed in Sheol, you are there.
⁹ *If I take the wings of the morning*
  and settle at the farthest limits of the sea,
¹⁰ *even there your hand shall lead me,*
  and your right hand shall hold me fast.
¹¹ *If I say, "Surely the darkness shall cover me,*
  and the light around me become night,"
¹² *even the darkness is not dark to you;*
  the night is as bright as the day,
  for darkness is as light to you.

^{13} *For it was you who formed my inward parts;*
*   you knit me together in my mother's womb.*
^{14} *I praise you, for I am fearfully and wonderfully made.*
*   Wonderful are your works;*
that I know very well.
^{15} *My frame was not hidden from you,*
when I was being made in secret,
*   intricately woven in the depths of the earth.*
^{16} *Your eyes beheld my unformed substance.*
In your book were written
*   all the days that were formed for me,*
*   when none of them as yet existed.*
^{17} *How weighty to me are your thoughts, O God!*
*   How vast is the sum of them!*
^{18} *I try to count them—they are more than the sand;*
*   I come to the end—I am still with you.*

(Psalm 139:1-18)

^{12}*After this he appeared in another form to two of them, as they were walking into the country.* ^{13}*And they went back and told the rest, but they did not believe them.*

(Mark 16:12-13)

^{16}*Now the eleven disciples went to Galilee, to the mountain to which Jesus had directed them.* ^{17}*When they saw him, they worshiped him; but some doubted.* ^{18}*And Jesus came and said to them, "All authority in heaven and on earth has been given to me.* ^{19}*Go therefore and make disciples of all nations, baptizing them in the name of the Father and of the Son and of the Holy Spirit,* ^{20}*and teaching them to obey everything that I have commanded you. And remember, I am with you always, to the end of the age."*

(Matthew 28:16-20)

This Jesus God raised up, and of that all of us are witnesses.

(Acts 2:32)

Session Guide

Welcome/Opening Prayer (5 minutes)

Welcome participants. You may wish to begin with prayer requests to include in the opening prayer, or you may save these for the closing prayer time.

Lead the group in an opening prayer, or ask a participant to pray. You may use your own prayer or the one below:

Lord Jesus, as you came alongside those two disciples on the road to Emmaus long ago, come alongside us today. Open our hearts that they may burn as you reveal yourself to each one of us. Remind us that you are the Lord of life. You have conquered the grave. You have called us to walk with you in faith, hope, and love. Inspire us with your word today so that we may recognize your presence with us. In Jesus' name. Amen.

Opening Activity (5 minutes)

Ask participants to tell about a time a friend or family member surprised them by coming to be with them for a special occasion, or "just because." How did it make them feel?

Reflect (25–40 minutes)

You will want to encourage participants to refer to the Reflect section at the end of the chapter during this time.

 *Historical Marker (5–10 minutes)*

Read or ask a group member to read Luke 24:13-35, followed by the contextual background of these verses found on pages 105–106 of *The Road to Amazing*. You may wish to share more background about this particular Scripture (see "Biblical Foundation," pages 53–54).

Ask group members to share their responses to the question in this section:

Where has Jesus surprised you by "showing up" on your faith journey?

 *Points of Interest (15–25 minutes)*

Summarize each of the sections below, pausing after each summary to ask group members to share the insights they listed in their books. Discuss why the insights were significant to them and ask how these insights will be applied in daily living.

• *The Road to Amazing*

Summary: Luke tells us that on that first Easter day, two of the disciples, one named Cleopas and the other not mentioned by name, were walking from Jerusalem to a village called Emmaus, about seven miles from Jerusalem. As he walks alongside them, he asks questions, listens, encourages them with the promises of the Scriptures, challenges them to have faith, until finally their eyes are open to the presence of Jesus with them, made known to them in the breaking of the bread.

Other notes:

Discuss the following:

- What insights did you record in your books?
- Why were these insights significant to you?
- How can you apply these insights in your daily living?

- *Jesus Comes Alongside the Broken*

Summary: God has a way of showing up when life has dealt us a blow. Life has a way of getting us down, but it is a sin to stay in that place and refuse to see that God is with us to help us through those times. Jesus comes along and enters into the conversation with us, even though we may not recognize at first that he is with us.

Other notes:

Discuss the following:

- What insights did you record in your books?
- Why were these insights significant to you?
- How can you apply these insights in your daily living?

- *Jesus Encourages the Discouraged*

Summary: Sometimes our best sight is hindsight. As we go through life, we are often unaware of the many ways

God walks with us and encourages us along the journey. When we look back across the years of our lives, we often find that there are many people God has placed along our paths who have given us support and encouragement.

Other notes:

Discuss the following:

- What insights did you record in your books?
- Why were these insights significant to you?
- How can you apply these insights in your daily living?

- *Jesus Brings New Life*

Summary: The road to amazing tells us there is a love that you can nail it to a tree and bury in a tomb, but it will never die. The same God who raised his Son, Jesus Christ, will raise us up with him also—nothing can ever separate us from this great love. We are resurrection people. We recognize and experience the realities of death, the Good Fridays of this world. But we know there is more to the story.

Other notes:

Discuss the following:

- What insights did you record in your books?
- Why were these insights significant to you?
- How can you apply these insights in your daily living?

 Souvenir (5 minutes)

Invite participants to share their answers to the question *What "souvenir" will you take with you as a remembrance of this chapter?* and tell why this was especially meaningful to them. Be prepared to share your own answer first if necessary.

Wrap Up (5 minutes)

As you come to the end of this study, thank the group for their participation over these four sessions. If you will be facilitating future studies (in The Basics series or another study), invite them to be a part and note the date when the study will begin.

Closing Prayer (5 minutes)

Encourage group members to continue remembering one another and the prayer requests that have been shared in their prayers.

Lead the group in prayer. You may pray the one provided, offer one of your own, or invite a participant to pray. If prayer requests were shared at the beginning, remind the group to include these in their daily prayer time in the coming week. Or invite prayer requests at this time and include them in the prayer. Another option is to invite everyone to recite the Lord's Prayer (Matthew 6:9-13).

Lord, the journey with you truly is the road to amazing. As we close this time together, remind us that you go with us. You have promised in your Word to be with us always. Even when we are not aware of it, you are there with us. Thank you, dear Lord. Walk with us as we go forward into the future. There are so many people in the world who think they are alone, without help. Send us out to proclaim the good news to others, that you have come for them and are with them. Help us invite them to join you on the road to amazing. We pray this prayer in the precious name of Jesus. Amen.

Extra Material for an Extended Session

Extra Activities

- Ask participants to tell about a trip or journey where they encountered an unexpected but welcome surprise.
- Ask participants to look up and read Scriptures from the Additional Scriptures section. You may wish to write the list of Scriptures on a chalkboard or on individual pieces of paper to distribute.

Extra Discussion Questions

- Have you had an experience where the "road to Emmaus" became the "road to amazing" for you?
- How has Jesus "showed up" when you were in times of grief and sorrow?

Notes for the Session

NOTES

1. William Arndt, F. Wilbur Gingrich, Frederick W. Danker, and Walter Bauer. *A Greek-English Lexicon of the New Testament and Other Early Christian Literature: A Translation and Adaptation of the Fourth Revised and Augmented Edition of Walter Bauer's Griechisch-Deutsches Wörterbuch Zu Den Schriften Des Neuen Testaments Und Der Übrigen Urchristlichen Literatur*. (Chicago: University of Chicago Press, 1979), 764.

2. "Luke," Professor J. A. Findlay, *The Abingdon Bible Commentary* (Garden City, NY: Doubleday & Company, Inc., 1929, 1957), 1041.

CPSIA information can be obtained
at www.ICGtesting.com
Printed in the USA
LVOW04s1120120116
469939LV00004B/22/P